Retirement SOLUTIONS
For
SMART PEOPLE™
HOW TO ACCOMPLISH FINANCIAL COMFORT

by,
Author & Photographer,
Manny Kagan

ENCOUNTERS
PUBLISHING

ISBN: 978-0-9971861-4-7

LCCN: 2023915977

Photography by: Manny Kagan

Cover design by: Jeni Shindorf

Library of Congress Control Number: 2018675309

Printed in the United States of America

To Elfa; beacon of my life

TABLE OF CONTENTS

INTRODUCTION

Many people would like to retire, but how many of us are actually ready to do so? In my forty years of helping clients improve their financial well-being through locating the right mortgage solutions, I have encountered only a few people who have enough financial resources to enjoy their lives without the need to generate additional employment income or rely on Social Security. Through online research I discovered that baby boomers in the United States, the people who were born between 1946 and 1964, amount to approximately 75 million people. By 2030, the number of baby boomers ready to retire in California alone is expected to reach more than 8 million. However, with the cost of living increasing every year, the retirement picture for these people could look rather bleak. Those fortunate enough to own their homes or condominiums might hold an advantage, due to the accumulation of equity as a result of paying down their mortgages and the appreciation of their properties over time. But regardless of people's situations, I decided to write this book, titled Retirement Solutions for Smart People. My hope being that, upon reading it, you will gain an understanding of at least one possible retirement solution. While it goes without saying that a number of solutions for a comfortable retirement exist, I focus specifically on one of them in this book— reverse mortgage. Surprisingly, when I talk with some of my clients about a reverse mortgage, I find that many of them react negatively. A primary concern among most people is that the bank will take away their house. It's a misconception based on rumors and misinformation; one that I am planning to dispel in this book But before we get into that, we first will learn some basic rules of the mortgage business, which I call the mortgage game. Acquiring a basic understanding of this game will equip you with the know-how needed to deal with lenders and ultimately, increase your chances of loan approval. Additionally, I will also guide you through the many different programs you can choose from depending on your needs and personal circumstances. To highlight the unique strengths of each program, I will share some of my clients' stories, showing you how they enjoyed their retirement after entering into a reverse mortgage or finding another mortgage solution. These stories will serve as real life examples, illustrating the possibilities and outcomes that can be achieved when selecting the right approach for the right situation. According to a survey conducted by the American Association of Retired People (AARP), 89 percent of survey responders said that they had a more comfortable lifestyle with the reverse mortgage and 87 percent felt that it improved their quality of life. Of all the borrowers, 94 percent said they felt that the reverse mortgage had given them peace of mind. Evidently, I do not have hundreds of thousands of people to survey, but I am sure that the clients whom I have helped, would answer that they have had a 100 percent satisfactory experience in each category.

CHAPTER 1

Our Story

Before we dive deeper into our reverse mortgage topic, I would like to share with you some information about my family.

I met my wife, Elfa, in the capital city of Latvia, Riga. Both of us were born there and got married when we were twenty. In January 1972, four members of our family—Elfa, myself, our daughter, and my wife's mother—immigrated to Israel. At the time, Elfa and I were twenty-five. As our life journey continued, a few years later in August 1980, we came to San Francisco with the addition of our second daughter, who had been born in Israel.

During my time in Riga, I studied industrial engineering, so while living in Israel, I worked as a project manager managing the construction of industrial plants. We came to San Francisco to further advance our education. Elfa studied fashion design, while I pursued an MBA degree. We did not have definite plans for our future; we just followed our life's path. I became a mortgage broker in 1983, and in 1985 Elfa and I established Pacific Bay Financial Corporation. We're still running the business together today, and on August 8, 2023 we celebrated our fifty-sixth wedding anniversary. The reason I share this with you is to point out that all of us have lifelong journeys, and retirement does not mean the end of the road. Being seventy-six, I definitely could retire. Instead, I keep going because my work and my life are about assisting others to have better lives. I feel that this is what I do in my day-to-day mortgage services. However, the solution to how to help those who want to retire and lack income, came after I "discovered" reverse mortgage.

Igor and Margarita

About eight years ago, a couple was referred to me by their real estate agent. Igor was eighty-two, and Margarita was seventy-three. After renting a small house for seventeen years, they were facing eviction because the owner had decided to sell the home. Of course, they could have just found another place to rent, however, rents were going up, and their income from Social Security and a small pension was about $20,000 a year. Fortunately, during their working days, they had saved $170,000. Now I had a challenge. They had been told "If Manny doesn't know how to help you, nobody will." What could I do? I had to find a solution. I knew that there was one mortgage program that I had not used until then, called "reverse mortgage". I also had heard that these programs were used to refinance existing mortgages. Could they be used for a purchase? As often happens in my life, answers present themselves. Around that time, I met Harold, who worked for a mortgage bank specializing in reverse mortgages. To cut a long story short, this proved to be the solution. My clients found a three-bedroom house, surrounded by mature fruit trees, in Pittsburg, California, which is a forty-minute ride on BART from San Francisco. Margarita's son, his wife, and their son also moved in. Every year Igor brings me a huge bag filled with prunes and oranges from their *backyard. Last year I refinanced their reverse mortgage into another one, lowering their interest rate.*

Through my many years in the mortgage business, I learned a lot about how to assist people by being aware of and using different options. Since I was becoming an expert, I wrote two mortgage-related books. We find a solution for most of our clients' mortgage needs so often that as a result, some of the people affectionately call me a miracle worker. What I do is not a miracle; rather it's the result of gaining knowledge about various mortgage tools and how to use them.

There are many advantages to reverse mortgages, especially for homeowners who may be challenged making their monthly payments. Other borrowers may need money for various purposes and although they may be able to make their monthly payments, they cannot qualify for a conventional mortgage, which would enable them to receive the cash they need. You will learn about these alternatives from the clients' stories that I am going to share in the pages ahead.

Buying real estate with a reverse mortgage might be challenging during a sellers' market when real estate agents write contracts with unrealistic closing timelines, and everyone is rushed. Getting a reverse mortgage can take time regardless of the market, especially since California has a seven-day cooling-off period built into the process.

Before we explore reverse mortgages, let's understand what a mortgage is.

CHAPTER 2

What is a Mortgage?

A mortgage is a loan that is secured, or guaranteed, using a piece of real estate as collateral. Most people, if given a choice, would rather not have a loan, but only a few of us have enough money to buy real estate with cash. To clarify, the word mortgage comes from Old French and literally means "dead pledge" (mort=dead, gage=pledge). One of the explanations for the word is that the agreement dies when the loan is paid off, or the borrower cannot make payments. In the latter case, whoever owns the note, can sell the property to recover the debt. A mortgage is actually a financial document that outlines the boundaries of the property that is to be used as collateral. Another important document in the many pages of the loan package is the note, which specifies the amount of the loan, the terms of repayment, the interest rate, and the monthly payments.

The term Mortgage can be misleading, especially since it is used in only twenty-five states. The rest of the states, including California, use a document called Deed of Trust. Many states allow the use of either document. Regardless, the word mortgage became synonymous with the industry.

I started in the mortgage industry in 1983, working for the mortgage bank Coldwell Financial. Mortgage banking was rare at that time, since the majority of the lenders were either commercial banks or savings and loans. While working for Coldwell, I started developing relationships with other lenders. Thus, coincidentally, I became one of the first mortgage brokers, because that same year Congress enacted the Secondary Mortgage Enhancement Act of 1983. This act created the opportunity for Wall Street to offer mortgage-backed securities and for the lenders to sell loans on the secondary market, thus raising more money to offer as mortgages. This in turn established underwriting guidance for lenders to evaluate, or qualify, potential borrowers. I described this process in my first book, "The Mortgage Game. The 5 C's and How to Connect Them". I call these guidelines the five C's: Collateral, Capacity, Credit, Cash (or Capital), and Character.

Let's look at each of them to see how they are interconnected. First off, lenders need collateral to protect their investment. Having collateral insures lenders that if something goes wrong (such as borrowers' not paying property taxes and insurance in the reverse mortgages) they will be able to recover some of the money lent to the borrower by selling the property. Collateral is created by the capital or cash invested at the beginning of the purchase transaction. The collateral is measured by the loan-to-value, or LTV. This in turn relates to the credit, which is measured by the borrowers' credit score, which relates to the capacity, or the ability, to make payments on time. Collateral is constantly changing as borrowers pay down the balance of the conventional mortgage. It is also influenced by the fluctuations of the economy. Over time, however, values often go up, thus protecting the collateral.

What lenders consider collateral; borrowers call equity. Usually, equity is calculated by subtracting the balance of the mortgage from the estimated value of the property. Because most reverse mortgages are refinancing transactions, the final loan amount is established after the appraisal is finished and accepted by the lender. As I mentioned before, capacity is the ability to make mortgage payments and meet other obligations, such as credit cards and car payments, on time. The advantage of a reverse mortgage is that even if a client's capacity goes down, such as when borrowers retire, he or she still can be qualified with a limited income. Credit is an important part of our lives, since it defines our paying habits and, in turn, affects our ability to get a mortgage. One's credit worthiness is defined by credit scores, known as FICO Scores, which are less important in reverse mortgages.

The combination of the first four c's creates the character of the mortgage and determines which lender(s) can offer the loan.

CHAPTER 3

What is a Reverse Mortgage?

A reverse mortgage is a special loan secured on an owner-occupied property, which gives the borrower the opportunity to skip the monthly payments. To understand why lenders offer these seemingly risky reverse mortgages, let's take a look at who the players are. When I worked on my first reverse mortgage, Harold, who had been involved with reverse mortgages for more than fifteen years, told me that majority of the borrowers are not qualified to get reverse mortgage because there is not enough equity in their property. At that time, most of the reverse mortgages were offered by the Federal Housing Administration (FHA), a government agency, which had pre-set, conforming loan limits that change every year. This meant that if borrowers needed a mortgage for an amount greater than these limits, they were not eligible. Gradually, as in other parts of the mortgage business that were dominated by the government-owned agencies such as FHA, Fannie Mae, and Freddie Mac, more lenders got into the field. This created what we have today; competitive lending opportunities.

There are two basic categories of reverse mortgages available to borrowers: (1) a home equity conversion mortgage (HECM), offered by FHA, i.e., by the federal government, and (2) a jumbo mortgage, offered by private parties through the mortgage banking companies. The major differences between these two types of reverse mortgage are the loan amount, the variety (fixed or adjustable loans or lines of credit) of the loans, and the costs. To find out which programs will offer better terms for borrowers, the loan originator has to understand clients' needs and collect basic information. The basic information includes the name of the borrowers, their birthdates, the property's estimated value (which can be checked online), and the current balance on the mortgage, if there is one. This information is inputted into a computer, and specially designed software will show available options.

Reverse mortgages have a number of rules, any of which, can affect the final outcome. For example, if the applicants are a couple, the loan amount is going to be based on the age of the younger applicant. Even so, the borrowers do not have to be married. Recently I helped a pair of clients (two men), who owned a house in which they lived as roommates. Nevertheless, both were reverse mortgage applicants. Though the calculation of the loan amount was based on the younger person's age, if his friend were to pass away first, the younger man would continue to live in the house without worrying about mortgage payments until the end of his days or until he might decide to sell the house. If a couple is married, then the same rule will apply: the surviving spouse can keep living in the house under the same terms, without the need to refinance. However, in the case where the couple is married but the property belongs to only one of them, these circumstances will require special solutions.

Paul

I had been assisting Paul for many years by refinancing mortgages on his home. He was eighty and still working part-time when he came to me to refinance again. This time, we ran into a problem. The issue was that since he was self-employed, his tax returns did not report enough income to qualify for the conventional loan. However, there was no problem in getting a reverse mortgage. He was married but had been separated from his wife for twenty years. His wife owned her own house but did not own his, i.e., her name was not on the title. Despite being separated, his wife had to sign an interspousal deed, prepared by the escrow company, to confirm that she has no interest in his property. This is a common situation where one of the spouses has to sign a quit claim deed for a conventional loan.

As it turns out, the rules were more complex for reverse mortgages, and I had to learn the specifics on the go. First, an attorney had to read the declaration to Paul's wife, and that exchange needed to be recorded on video and notarized. Since this situation occurred before COVID-19, I was able to arrange a meeting at the escrow company in Oakland, California, where Paul's wife lived and worked, as did the attorney I hired for this process. Everything seemed straightforward. The wife was able to come during her lunch, the attorney did his part, and I recorded it with my mobile phone. After an escrow officer notarized the affidavit, we forwarded everything to the lender. However, our submission was not acceptable, as I had missed two steps. With reverse mortgages, I learned that lenders want to be protected. In this case, that meant they wanted to make sure that each spouse was properly informed. To satisfy their requirements, I had to hire a court reporter and a professional videographer and bring everyone together again, including the attorney. All of this made the wife, who had cancer, upset. As a result, I wanted to put the whole reverse mortgage business on hold, but my client needed money; some of which he needed for home repairs. I am not in the reverse mortgage business, but rather I am in the business of finding mortgage solutions, so of course I found one for Paul. I knew that in the event of my client's death, the property was going to be inherited by the couple's son. The wife was still working, and I asked if she would be willing to assist Paul. Her income combined with her husband's was enough to qualify for a conventional mortgage. Later, if his wife were to pass before him, we might consider getting a reverse mortgage to get rid of the monthly payments.

Reverse mortgages can help many retirees, but often there are other possible solutions. My skills as a mortgage broker have helped many borrowers who wanted to retire. One of my former clients, specializes in reverse mortgages. When he could not offer a client reverse mortgage solutions, he would refer that client to me. In one case, a couple wanted to move into a retirement community. They owned two properties that they did not want to sell. One of the properties was already rented, and they planned to rent the second one as well to generate income after moving to their new home. They did, however, need to have enough money to buy into the retirement community. Since reverse mortgages can be secured only for owner-occupied properties, I instead used a conventional mortgage with a low interest rate to help them get the extra money needed to buy a home in the retirement community. Unfortunately, not everyone who needs mortgage help can receive it. Typically, this is due to a lack of equity in the property, which is determined by the appraisal report.

Bob and Angela

I have a very good friend, Bob, who for many years was a high-ranking executive at a major U.S. corporation. As a troubleshooter, he traveled the world, and his family was well off. When he retired, he and his wife relied on his social security, small pension, and their investments. When Angela was diagnosed with an unusual type of cancer, the doctors gave her three months to live. To beat the odds, they used their savings on new experimental drugs. Ultimately, the cancer was gone, but so was their money. I was happy to help them by securing a reverse mortgage. As a result, they were able to choose not to have mortgage payments and had another $200,000 to ease their retirement.

Two years later, Bob called back, wondering if he could get more money. He and his wife were older, and the property value had gone up. According to the computer software program we use, the answer was "Yes." How much money he could get depended on the appraisal report. A local real estate agent who wanted to get business was sending them information that he could list the property for $2.5 million. But when we ordered an appraisal report, the results showed the value as $2.2 million. That in turn, created a new situation. When the property value is *appraised at more than $2 million, lenders require a second appraisal report. This was during the time when interest rates were low and appraisers were very busy. Two months later, a second appraisal report indicated the property value at $1.8 million. Appraisers are human beings, so they express their opinions based on personal experience, familiarity with the area, how busy they are, and their willingness to take the time to do thorough research. However, since lenders use the lower of two appraisals, the $1.8 million was not enough to get my clients the necessary loan amount.*

I decided to order a third appraisal report. Since the first lender would not consider the new value, we also had to switch to a different bank and to apply for a different loan. To my relief and my clients' benefit, the new appraisal came in at $2 million. That meant that there was no need for the second appraisal report with the lower valuation, and then the loan was approved. When I visited Bob and Angela six months later, he told me that the house next door, which was identical to his, had just sold for $2.6 million. This sale will make a good comp when someone in the area next needs an appraisal for mortgage financing.

As you can see from Bob's story, a property's value, which defines collateral (the first of the five C's), can be very "flexible" but it has a significant role in defining the loan amount and therefore, the success of the transaction. The value of the property, which is established by the appraisal report, is probably the most challenging aspect of any mortgage transaction, as we will see in the next case.

John and Tom

Another of my recent reverse mortgage situations involved a property that had been inherited by three men. When one of the men got sick, he wanted to sell his 33 percent to take care of his health. As it happens, the property had no current mortgage on it, and the remaining two heirs, John and Tom, were planning to stay on the property for the foreseeable future. So, my task was to secure a $1.2 million cash-out loan so that my clients could pay off the third partner. Both borrowers had limited income and were more than sixty-two years old, so the solution was a reverse mortgage.

The property was a unique, large Victorian house built in 1896. The first step in getting the loan was to do some fixing and painting. I introduced the men to a handyman, and when the work was done and they had completed the obligatory counseling about what a reverse mortgage involves, we ordered an appraisal report. Since the value had to come in over $3 million, we needed two appraisal reports. The first one was done relatively quickly, and the property was appraised for $5.5 million. For the second one, we waited more than three months, which made everyone upset. When we finally received the second report, it showed the property's value as $3.8 million. Although that's a huge difference when compared to the value listed in the first appraisal, in this case it did not matter. The lender used the lower value, but it still was enough to get the necessary loan amount.

As we just saw, when it comes to property appraisals, everything depends on the appraiser's opinion and experience. In the end, the appraisal will establish how much of a reverse mortgage borrowers will be able to get. As we know, the value of a property is defined by many factors. One of those factors is the oldest rule in the book: "Location, location, location,"; which means that the appraisal report for similar properties in different locations, will define the selling price. For "comps" (comparable) the estimated value is determined by the availability of comparisons. These "comps" provide information on similar properties sold near the property that is being evaluated. Sales included in the comps must have been completed within a specific recent time period. Since many properties used in comps differ from one another, appraisers use adjustments, such as: numbers of rooms and bathrooms, presence of a garage, the property's condition, and the view; to compensate for the increasing or decreasing of the value accordingly. When there are mistakes or discrepancies, appraisal results can be disputed, but doing so is often a waste of time. Appraisal reports are ordered by the lenders from one of the appraisal management companies (AMCs) to avoid any outside influence on the outcome.

Besides comparisons, another critically important factor in determining property value is the condition of the property. For reverse mortgages, a property cannot have peeling paint, the boiler must be double strapped to the wall for safety, and every room or space, including the garage, needs to have smoke and CO2 detectors in place. Though clutter inside the property is not supposed to affect the value, it might have a personal effect on the appraisers. Also, what is to be done if the property needs repairs, but the borrowers don't have the money to do them? One of the possible solutions is to look into getting a loan from the private lender; the so-called "hard money loan". Regulators have set up restrictions on these loans, and as a result, many lenders do not want to mess with them. This can make it challenging to get a private loan on an owner-occupied property. Recently, I've discovered that reverse mortgages can also offer "set asides", money to fix a property.

Roger

This very issue came to light when I tried to help Roger, a client who needed in-home support that was costing him $8,000 every month. Roger's property was owned free and clear, so he did not have a mortgage, but he also did not have sufficient income to qualify for a conventional loan. When I went for a visit, I found a number of other issues affecting his ability to get financing. Most important among these was his mental capacity—he had dementia. Fortunately, Roger's former girlfriend had durable power of attorney, and this allowed her to deal with his money.

The condition of his property was another issue. The house needed repainting, its broken windows needed to be replaced, and Roger needed to get rid of the clutter that had accumulated in every room. I knew contractors who could do the work, but the issue was finding the money to pay for them. Where was it going to come from? This is when I really came to understand the challenges of getting a private loan, which included getting the client counseling similar to what one receives for a reverse mortgage. In this case, considering Roger's mental condition, it was his former girlfriend who needed to receive reverse mortgage counseling.

As I noted earlier, it often happens in my life that when I am faced with a problem, an unexpected solution presents itself. In this case, I received an e-mail from a friend who specializes in reverse mortgages; He wrote about a lender who offers money in exchange for a percentage of the property's future value. There was no need to have income to qualify, and there would be no monthly payments. The program is called home equity investment (HEI); which I will discuss in greater detail later. It seemed to be the perfect solution. I suggested he apply for a $200,000 HEI. This amount would give the client six months' worth of in-home support payments as well as enough cash to fix the property and pay the service providers. This would leave Roger with enough money for a rainy day. The original plan was that once the property was fixed, we would apply for a reverse mortgage. Once that was secured, the $200,000 plus the agreed-upon interest would be repaid. During these negotiations, Roger's condition worsened, he had to be moved into an assisted living facility, and therefore could not get a reverse mortgage since to qualify, the property must be owner occupied. By this time, his former girlfriend now lived in the house. Unfortunately, the HEI lenders decided that they were unable to work with her power of attorney. Since his need for money was still there, we came to a very simple solution. The girlfriend wrote a letter to the Lender stating that she was a tenant of Roger's property, thus making the property a rental property. As a result, the private lender had no problem providing a hard-money loan.

Fred

I met Fred in a restaurant where he worked as a host. For years, that restaurant was our favorite place to go before attending symphony concerts. We were "regulars" and never had problems getting a reservation and even had "our" table by the window. From our many visits, Fred knew that I'm a mortgage broker, and one evening, he asked if I would review his mortgage statement. I did so. After the review, I reported back to him that he had a good mortgage and that there was no need to do anything right now. A few years later, Fred told me about his plans to retire. I asked if he would be able to afford his mortgage payment in retirement and suggested he take a look at reverse mortgages. It took Fred a year before he called me back. His thinking, he explained, was that since he had no children, he was planning to leave his home to charity after he was gone. Until that happened, he wanted to enjoy his life without thinking about the mortgage payments, therefore a reverse mortgage was a perfect choice for him.

A reverse mortgage can help people in many instances, however in the case of an inheritance a reverse mortgage could become the only solution.

Mike

Mike was referred to me by an estate attorney after his aunt Mary's death. Fortunately for Mike, his aunt bequeathed her house to him. Which was perfect since he was already living in the house. Of course, the property had to be transferred to his name, which would not be challenging since Aunt Mary had a trust and Mike was her beneficiary. The problem was that there was a mortgage on the house that had to be paid off. Mike was handicapped and arrived for an appointment at my office in a wheelchair. Because of his age and physical challenges, there was a very simple solution: a reverse mortgage. The reverse mortgage paid off the existing mortgage, eliminating any mortgage payment for Mike, and he received a check for more than $300,000. This additional cash meant he could afford to hire someone to assist him. Sometimes reverse mortgages can help people in unexpected ways.

As I mentioned before, one of the major misconceptions I hear about reverse mortgages is that a bank can seize a property after the owner's death. As we have seen before, the reverse mortgage, just like a conventional mortgage, is the loan secured (guaranteed) by the property. When a person dies, the property goes to one's heirs, whether family members, friends, or a charity. If there is an existing reverse mortgage, the loan has to be paid off within six months, with the possibility of an additional extension for another six. During this time property can be either sold or refinanced, as you will find out in my next story.

Dave and Hanna

Dave and Hanna inherited a small house, where they lived together with their daughter and their dog. The house had a reverse mortgage, which Hanna's deceased father, who lived in the house, had taken out a number of years before his death. On the surface, the situation surrounding the house was relatively simple: refinance the loan. As it turned out, Dave had medical issues and lost his job. His wife also required medical attention and their daughter worked at a fast-food restaurant and earned minimum wage. The family's combined income was not enough to qualify for a new conventional mortgage, and I struggled to find a solution for them. Then it dawned on me: Dave was going to be sixty-two in three months, which meant that he could qualify for a reverse mortgage. Even with that as a solution, we faced a number of issues. One, I needed to secure an extension for paying off the existing reverse mortgage and two, was the condition of the property. As it stood, the house would not be acceptable for a reverse mortgage due to the repairs needed. To fix the property, I was able to arrange for a private loan, which was also challenging, since, as I mentioned before, there are restrictions on offering private loans on owner-occupied properties, but when the dust settled, the new reverse mortgage replaced the previous one.

Most people are concerned with who will inherit their property after they are gone; however, some people have figured out how to use the equity in their homes for good causes even while they are still alive. One of my clients used a reverse mortgage with cash-out to pay for a grandson's college tuition. It gave my clients great satisfaction to be able to do this and also not have to worry about the monthly payments.

Clara

I've known Clara for more than thirty-five years. She used to sell real estate, and we worked together with many of her clients. At the same time, she was my client as well. As the years progressed, Clara decided that she had sold real estate long enough, and she retired. She owned and lived in a two-unit building, so besides social security, she was also receiving rent, but even with those two streams of income, Clara didn't have much left after her mortgage payments each month.

Every time I would mention a reverse mortgage, her response was always the same: "I am not interested." Nevertheless, she called me one day with a question, "What if I decide to get a reverse mortgage and then sell my property and move to a retirement community later on?"

I used an amortization table to show her what her accumulated balance on a reverse mortgage would be year after year, but the table also showed that, at the same time, the value of her property would continue to go up, so there was always going to be equity left over. In the meantime, she would be able to enjoy life with the extra money since she would no longer have a mortgage payment to worry about.

Two years after Clara took out a reverse mortgage, she called again. "Can I refinance and pull out some cash?" she asked. "I want to help my niece while I am still alive." It was a relatively easy process since she was advanced in age and the property value had already gone up significantly.

Clara was among those of my clients who, after getting their first reverse mortgage, could refinance it into another reverse mortgage eighteen months later.

John and Greta

Before retirement, John and Greta managed their company together for more than forty years. During those years, I refinanced their mortgage a number of times. When the business ran into financial difficulty, especially since both of them were older by then, they decided to retire. Unfortunately for them, the house they owned had both a mortgage and a line of credit on it, totaling $900,000. By this time, their income was limited to social security and mandatory distributions from their retirement accounts. This was not enough to maintain the lifestyle they were accustomed to. Selling their house did not make sense. For one thing, they would have had to pay significant capital gain tax on the sale; for another, they did not want to move.

Greta called me for advice and I suggested a reverse mortgage as a possible solution. After an appraisal was done, they discovered that the amount of the reverse mortgage they could get was only $750,000. They then consulted with their children and decided to use $150,000 from their retirement accounts to pay the difference.

I wasn't expecting to hear from them again since it seems a reverse mortgage is often the last mortgage a property owner needs. Nevertheless, two years later, I received a call. John and Greta needed my advice again. They had sold their office building and found that they owed the government $150,000 in taxes. In the two years since we talked, a number of things had changed. They were older, to be sure, but also the value of their home had increased. I checked their numbers on the computer software. During this period, they did not make monthly mortgage payments and the balance was increased. Despite that, we could refinance and pay Internal Revenue Service.

While reverse mortgages can help a lot of people during their retirement, they are not right for everyone. Some potential borrowers won't qualify for this mortgage and still others do not see how it can benefit them.

Margy

Eighty-year-old Margy was referred to me by the owner of an in-home support company that provided her with twenty-four-hour care. When I went for a visit, I discovered she was mostly bedridden, and from her bed, she spent her time watching TV, sleeping, and talking on the phone.

In a nutshell, her finances looked like this: Her in-home support service costs her $200,000 a year, but the house, which she had inherited from her sister, was mortgage free. It seemed to me that she would probably be better off selling the house and moving into a retirement community with medical supervision. When she said she was not ready for that, I suggested getting about $800,000 in a *reverse mortgage. This would carry her for about four years. She decided against it. When I checked with her a year later, she was residing at an assisted living facility.*

CHAPTER 4

How it Works

By now you've read quite a few personal stories and are probably ready to find out about what it takes to get a reverse mortgage.

Every borrower starts the same way. After the clients' information is entered into the computer, the software shows different reverse mortgage scenarios. According to the rules, every offer needs to have the FHA loan options, even if the loan originator knows that the solution that can best meet the clients' needs is probably a jumbo loan.

While FHA loans are the same for every lender, the jumbo loans offer different features. After the loan originator discusses options with a client, a preliminary three-page proposal outlining various choices as well as an amortization schedule is emailed, mailed or presented in person to the borrowers. After the client chooses the most suitable option, she or he receives a full proposal package that contains a list of counselors, as well as documents describing what a reverse mortgage is. The next step is to connect with one of the counselors and spend close to an hour on the phone talking about reverse mortgages (at a cost of about $150.00 charged to the client's credit card). Then the counselor issues a confirmation certificate, which is emailed to the loan originator. If the borrower lives in California, everyone then waits for seven days, which is the mandatory cooling-off period. Only then can the appraisal report be ordered and loan application containing over 200 pages is sent to the client. The loan amount is set only after an appraisal is done and accepted. At this point, the final interest rate is locked, and the process is complete.

When interest rates suddenly jumped—as they did in the middle of 2022—lenders changed the formula to compensate for the increase. As a result, two of my clients could not get the loans they wanted because the lendable amounts were reduced.

James

James, who was introduced to me by a mutual friend, wanted to borrow one million dollars in cash from the equity of his house, but he had been turned down by the major bank where he was a client. At the same time, because of his age and property value, he was qualified to get $800,000 through a reverse mortgage. That was good news, but unfortunately, while we were processing his loan, the interest rate rose from 4.5 percent to 8.5 percent, and the approved loan amount went down significantly, so James decided not to take the smaller loan.

Increases in the mortgage interest rate in 2022 and 2023 created a lot of challenges. Conventional refinancing stopped overnight, qualifying for purchases became more difficult, and reverse mortgages stopped making sense for many borrowers.

Wendy

We started refinancing Wendy's existing reverse mortgage in April 2022. About two years earlier, I had arranged her first reverse mortgage. This first reverse mortgage had perfect timing since, due to illness, Wendy was having difficulty working. The ongoing pandemic at the time only served to make things worse. The original refinancing plan was to follow the same process we had gone through before, i.e., to refinance with cash out and maintain the same interest rate. It was possible since the value of Wendy's home had increased significantly.

However, now that the home was worth $2.5 million, the lender required additional appraisal reports. (The second appraisal came in at $2.4 million.) Then there was another issue: Wendy owned the building where her business was operating and her business was reporting negative cash flow, which affected her ability to qualify. It took us four months to get to the finish line and by that time, interest rates had gone up, so the process was over. We will wait for interest rates to come down before revisiting her need for more money.

CHAPTER 5

A Line of Credit

Borrowers can benefit from the equity accumulated in their properties in a number of ways. One of the ways is to secure a line of credit (L/C). The most familiar lines of credit are offered by the commercial banks, credit unions, and specialty mortgage banks. These L/Cs are sometimes called second loans because they are recorded after the original mortgage. At the same time, reverse mortgage lines of credit are replacing an original loan, and they therefore become the first loan.

All L/Cs are adjustable loans, and therefore consist of two parts. The first part is the fluctuation of the index which makes the rate adjustable and the second part is a fixed margin or profit. By adding both together, you get the note rate, or the interest rate that borrowers are going to pay. One of the advantages of L/Cs is that borrowers have a source of funds that can be used when needed and paid back the balance to lower their monthly obligations. At least this is what every borrower hopes for when they take out an L/C. If this is not done after ten years, the L/C converts into a conventional loan and has to be paid off during the next twenty years. In the first ten years, the payment can be interest only, however, the last twenty years have to include principal as well. Thus, the payment can go higher, which can make it unaffordable. Conventional L/Cs are tied to the prime rate, which, until recently was relatively low since it is based on the federal funds rate. In April 2022, it was 0.5 percent, and a year later the Federal Reserve increased it to 5.50 percent. The prime rate is calculated by adding 3 percent to the federal funds rate. Thus, the prime rate is currently 8.50 percent and is expected to increase further. Recently, I read that, despite the current high prime rates, the use of lines of credit has increased significantly. The main reason is probably a lack of personal income. Until a year ago, when the conventional mortgage interest rate was less than 5 percent, it was common practice to consolidate debts through refinancing by combining a first loan with a line of credit.

Since the consolidation of two loans into a conventional mortgage is not feasible now, in November 2023 when I'm writing this, one possible solution is to wait until interest rates come down or, if possible, to refinance with a reverse mortgage.

Linda

Linda was seventy-five when the payment on her $177,000 line of credit went up to $2,500 per month. Her solution was to consolidate both loans into a reverse mortgage. As a result, after her monthly obligations were gone, she could also receive $52,177 in cash at closing and a $118,287 line of credit, which she can start using after a year. This was possible because of Linda's age and her property's appraisal value.

One of Linda's concerns was the cost of the process. (I will address this important issue in a separate chapter).

When the interest rates increased on every type of mortgage, the rates on a reverse mortgage L/C went up as well. Reverse mortgage lines of credit are tied not to the prime rate but, rather, to different indices, like a one-year Treasury bill, which is currently at 5.40 percent.

It is important to understand that when the index goes down, the adjustable rate follows. For example, at the end of 2022, it was 4.73%. However, in 2021, the one-year T-Bill was only 0.39%. Therefore, in the long run, adjustable L/Cs can be the better choice.

Reverse mortgage L/Cs have remarkable features. Unlike conventional L/Cs, they never expire. Additionally, the amount that is not used continues to grow tied to the interest plus mortgage insurance. It can also be paid down, further increasing the available funds.

Beatrice

Beatrice used to own an apartment in a tenancy in common (TIC) four-unit building. After the property was converted into four condominiums, I helped her arrange a mortgage for her unit. She sold the place six months later and used the profit to pay cash for a small house. Later on, she wanted to improve the property. By that time, she was retired and did not have enough income to qualify for a conventional mortgage or line of credit. However, since qualification for a reverse mortgage has less requirements, I arranged a reverse mortgage line of credit for her, which also does not involve monthly payments. She used some of the money to build an additional room and bathroom for her sister's visits.

Unfortunately, Beatrice died soon after the project was completed. Her children, who inherited the property, sold it for much more than the total of what she had originally paid for the place plus the cost of improvements.

This next story was told to me by my associate, Juan. He and I have been working together for more than thirty-six years and counting. He has many long term clients for whom he has refinanced mortgages a number of times over the years that we have been working together.

Natalie and George

When Natalie and her husband, George, reached their middle eighties, George fell off a ladder, hit his head, and died. Now a widow, Natalie had accumulated $80,000 in credit card debt. The original idea was to refinance an existing mortgage with the cash out to pay off the debts. But when she and Juan realized that her income was not enough to qualify for a conventional refinancing, he recommended getting a reverse mortgage line of credit instead. Natalie's son, who had been an attorney, objected. His argument was that she had $300,000 in savings. Juan's experience in dealing with hundreds of borrowers taught him that this amount might not be enough. Following Juan's recommendation, Natalie decided to get a reverse mortgage line of credit, which, because of her property's appraised value and the fact that she was eighty-two, amounted to $550,000.

CHAPTER 6

Reverse Mortgage Seconds

As I've mentioned before, the time of the recording of the mortgage makes it either the first or second (even in some instances third) mortgage. During the last few years, when interest rates were low, many borrowers purchased homes and condominiums with low interest rate mortgages. The same happened with the refinancing. In addition, many also got lines of credit, which, after ten years, became second mortgages with high interest rates and much higher monthly payments. Borrowers who have difficulty making high payments might have an alternative solution: a fixed rate Reverse Mortgage Second loan. It can be used as a separate second loan or to replace an existing L/C or second mortgage, as long as the first mortgage has a fully amortized fixed rate (not those which are fixed for a short period of time, such as 5 or 7 years). Reverse Mortgage Second does not have a monthly payment, and borrowers who are 55 and older are eligible. However, unlike a regular reverse mortgage, there is stricter underwriting criteria. The fixed interest rate is similar to other current second loans, or L/C, offered by the banks. It is relatively high, currently at 9.99%. However, if your first mortgage has a low interest rate and you need money or cannot make payments on your current L/C, it can be the perfect solution. Besides, the interest rate is lower than the rate on credit cards. You can pay off your other obligations, which have a higher rate, and have no monthly payments.

This option can serve as an alternative solution for those clients who have a first mortgage with a low interest rate and can afford to make monthly payments.

Steve

A few years ago, my colleague Mayya was helping her client Steve and arranging a refinancing of their forward mortgage with an interest rate of 2.875% and a current balance of about $474,000, which had monthly payments of $2,107. He could handle this payment, but he wanted to have some extra money for a "rainy day". When he applied for the line of credit with the local bank, he was told that he could qualify for only $35,000; however, the ban's minimum is loan amount is $50,000, therefore he couldn't get this second loan. After Mayya checked how much money Steve could qualify for with a reverse mortgage, she determined that after paying off the first mortgage, he could get extra cash out of $189,000. However, the new interest rate for the total loan amount, including the first mortgage, was 9.74%, which did not make any sense. Then she checked the reverse mortgage second. In this scenario, Steve could get $327,000 with an interest rate of 9.99% without losing the benefit of the first mortgages low interest rate. If he could afford to make payments on the first mortgage, this could be a very good option.

Of course, there are drawbacks. Since this is a reverse mortgage and not a line of credit, he needs to take out the whole amount at closing of the loan transaction.

To give you the right perspective, if he could get the line of credit from the bank, it would probably have the prime rate plus one percent, which is today equivalent to 9.50%, and may continue to grow.

Extra money can serve many different purposes. Some borrowers use reverse mortgage seconds for real estate investments, like buying a second home. One of our clients wanted to add an accessory dwelling unit (ADU) to his house to create a source of additional monthly income and a potential increase in the future value of the property. When he ran out of money to finish the project, he checked with me to see if he could get a reverse mortgage to get the extra money but unfortunately the value of the property had not increased enough for him to qualify.

CHAPTER 7

Home Equity Investment (HEI)

In some instances, clients cannot or do not want to take on a reverse mortgage. To assist them, a friend who specializes in reverse mortgages introduced me to an alternative program. It is called home equity investment (HEI). An HEI is not considered a loan; rather, it is an agreement between the property owner and the company that advances the property owner money. The process is relatively simple. There is no need to prove an income, and there are no age restrictions (unlike the reverse mortgage) but a higher credit score can have a positive effect on the amount of the agreement. The key to the program is a property's appraised value. After an appraisal report is done, a mortgage company deducts about 15 percent (the percentage can vary) from the value as a starting point. During the time of the homeownership, borrowers do not have to make payments (similar to reverse mortgages) however, when the property is sold or refinanced, the company uses the percentage of the future appreciation to calculate the amount owed by the borrower agreed in advance.

There are a number of companies that offer HEI-type loans or future equity share agreements. They vary, and therefore clients need to thoroughly review each offer before agreeing on an option. Sometimes the choice between a reverse mortgage and a home equity investment (HEI) depends on the type of property the borrower holds.

Nancy

I met Nancy a number of years ago through a friend. She wanted to slow down her private therapy practice but needed some money to fix her condominium. It seemed that a reverse mortgage was the right solution for her, but I encountered an issue that eliminated that option.

Reverse mortgages have several restrictions when it comes to condominium projects. The first of these is that the condominium project needs to have Federal Housing Administration (FHA) condo approval. Another consideration is the percentage of owner-occupiers on the property. Nancy owns a condominium in a four-unit building. To get an FHA loan, the building must be 75 percent owner-occupied. However, in her case, one couple occupies two units, which they combined into one large unit. As a result, it was not possible to get a reverse mortgage. I then looked into a jumbo reverse mortgage for her, only to find out that it had the same FHA condo guidance and restrictions.

When I mentioned the HEI program to the friend who had introduced us, he immediately responded, "Have you told Nancy about that program?" Yes, I did. This was the right choice for her. After the process was completed, based on the unit's appraised value, Nancy received enough money to pay off her existing mortgage and have some extra money as well. Ultimately, this had the same effect as a reverse mortgage would have; Nancy was able to enjoy her life without having to worry about mortgage payments.

Sometimes home equity investment (HEI) and reverse mortgage programs can complement each other, like in the following complicated case.

Andrey and Olga

Andrey was referred to me by a real estate agent who told me that Andrey and Olga wanted to buy a new property in Sacramento, California. Since he had limited income, Andrey would probably need a reverse mortgage. When I originally spoke with Andrey about six months ago, I wasn't sure how I could help him. He and his wife had some savings, and since Olga was younger than Andrey, we were calculating the amount of reverse mortgage they could get based on her age and the future $800,000 value, making the reverse mortgage loan amount about $300,000. Their original plan was to keep their condominium in Daly City, California, buy a new house, and only then sell their condo. In other words, they needed a bridge loan. We have several lenders who offer bridge loans, but the couple didn't have enough income to qualify.

When I forwarded the property address and the balance of the owners' current mortgage to an HEI company, I received a response saying that based on the estimated value and the combined loan-to-value (LTV) amount, the couple might be able to receive a net of about $170,000. Coupled with their savings, that would give them enough money to make a down payment on a new home and to qualify for the non-owner-occupied loan based on the rent payments only. Once the *couple sells the condominium, the amount leftover after paying off the existing mortgage plus the HEI agreement will give them extra money to lower the amount of their mortgage and be able to qualify for a reverse mortgage, which, as I calculated before, was $300,000. This would mean they never have to worry about making another mortgage payment again.*

This kind of transaction requires creativity and a deep knowledge of the mortgage business.

In some instances, borrowers can choose between a reverse mortgage and an HEI program.

Linda

Linda was referred to me by an attorney. On the phone, she told me that she wanted a reverse mortgage for her home because she was eighty years old and had medical issues. When we met, she arrived with her son. Based on my calculation, she could qualify for either $600,000 through a reverse mortgage or $300,000 through an HEI. Her son had chosen the HEI program. The advantage of an HEI program is that the borrower does not have to reside on the property to be eligible. Sometimes money is needed to move to an assisted living facility.

Regardless of which program is chosen, it is often a good idea to discuss the options with the children.

CHAPTER 8

Reverse Mortgages for Purchases

It took eight years after the first purchase transaction involving a reverse mortgage for Igor and Margarita, which I described at the beginning of this book, when I received the text message, "Are you still doing reverse mortgages?" It came from one of my former clients, Christine, who moved to Nevada.

Christine

When I called her back, Christine told me that she was tired of dealing with the snow in winter and would like to move back to California. "Where to?" I inquired. "Sacramento," she answered. "I want to sell our home in Nevada, use the money for the down payment, and get a reverse mortgage for balance."

Her destination surprised me, since some Californians move to Nevada to avoid high costs. What she said next surprised me even more. Christine sent me information about the house she wanted to buy, which was listed for $2,840,000. "I hope they will not sell it before I can buy it." She is sixty-eight, and her husband is ten years older. After I inputted her birthday and property price into the computer, it showed that she could get about $950,000 as a reverse mortgage. "Perfect", she said, "I am going to sell my Nevada home for over 2 million; since we have no mortgage, it is going to be enough for the down payment. What is the interest rate?" she inquired. "9.8%," I answered. "I don't care!" she exclaimed,

"As long as I am not going to have monthly payments. And if not that property; I will find another one."

This was not a typical scenario, since, as I pointed out, many people are downsizing and moving to less expensive areas of California or other states. Regardless of the destination, these reverse mortgages can be used in many states starting at age 55. However, the older you are, the more money you can get.

CHAPTER 9

Divorces and Reverse Mortgages

Divorce is probably one of the most stressful events in a person's life. It involves both emotional and financial issues. These can become more challenging as the couple reaches retirement age when their sources of income are diminishing, and they own real estate together. For over twenty years I have had the opportunity to help many couples while I was assisting a family-law attorney who was acting as mediator during friendly divorces. I had to find creative mortgage solutions, since usually one of the divorcees would end up with the home, while the other got the money. The main challenge was how to qualify for a mortgage for one person with limited income. This is not a problem with reverse mortgages, but the property value can be. This is especially true since interest rates have gone up and the loan-to-value, or the amount the borrower can get, has gone down. Nevertheless, reverse mortgages might still offer a solution. However, it has to be part of the divorce strategy, which can only be accomplished during the negotiations and requires the attorney's awareness. This is where I come in.

Robert

Robert was referred to me by a divorce attorney. After 22 years of marriage, he and his wife decided to take different journeys. They owned a house with a double *lot in a good part of San Francisco. For the purpose of divorce, it was appraised at $1,950,000. Based on that amount, Robert agreed to buy his wife out for $850,000. Since there was an existing mortgage of $375,000, he needed $1,225,000. Robert was sixty-seven, and next year he was planning to retire. His first question was, "Can I get a reverse mortgage?" Because of the high loan amount, it wasn't possible, however, after I analyzed his circumstances, I found a way for him to qualify for the needed loan amount., I offered him the following strategy: After he gets the house, he can sell the adjacent lot, pay down his new mortgage through refinancing with the reverse mortgage and use the money to lower the loan amount by refinancing with a reverse mortgage. Mission accomplished; he can retire, keep getting social security and rent from the in-law unit, and not have any mortgage payments.*

Some divorces face different challenges.

Caroline

Caroline is the stepdaughter of one of my clients. She was fifty-nine when her husband, Greg, filed for divorce. They stayed friends, and when she decided to buy him out, Greg agreed to help her get qualified for the conventional mortgage using his income. The divorce agreement stipulated that Greg's name would be taken out in three years. By that time, Caroline is going to be sixty-two, and I will refinance their old loan with a reverse mortgage and have only Caroline's name on the title.

Working with many clients who are going through divorce, I found out that what I think is right for people is not always necessarily the case.

Joan

Joan and her husband worked as event photographers for many years. When he filed for divorce, she was crushed. Eventually, Joan ended up with the house and the original mortgage, for which both incomes had been used to qualify. However, Joan could take out a reverse mortgage based on the property value and her age. It would be enough to pay off her current mortgage and she would have some extra cash. Not having a monthly payment would greatly help her cash flow; nevertheless, Joan ultimately decided against it, but it was her reason that surprised me. Joan explained that since she could still make a living as a photographer, taking a reverse mortgage would make her feel like a failure in her eyes.

You never know what motivates people's decisions.

CHAPTER 10

What About the Children

Before finishing this book about how retirees can benefit from reverse mortgages and other options, I need to bring another party to the table—adult children. Actually, reading the information about how to help one's parents retire is as important for the children as for the parents. Every situation is different. During my first meetings with clients, one of the questions I ask is if they have children or not. Recently, I visited a prospective client in an affluent area of San Francisco and asked the question about their children. The woman responded, "F--k the children." This couple did not become my clients.

In families where the relationship with their children is mutually beneficial, it is often the children who suggest that their parents get a reverse mortgage so that they can enter retirement without worry. Some care about their parents' well-being; for others, it is a more practical concern. Many people's budgets, especially if they have children of their own, do not allow them to take care of their parents' needs as well.

Greg and Jenny

Recently, one of our associates, Dwight, was helping clients Greg and Jenny refinance a five-unit building. The lender could not approve the loan request because of the clients' personal cash flow issues. Since both Greg and Jenny were more than sixty-two years old, one possible solution was to take out a reverse mortgage on their residence, pay off two existing mortgages, and improve their monthly cash flow. This solution made sense until they informed their daughter about it. She went ballistic, claiming that her parents had promised her their real estate as an inheritance. For twenty-five minutes, Dwight listened to her and then said that she was right. This took the wind out of her sails. Dwight then proceeded to explain to her the strategy of the transaction. After she understood that the result of the reverse mortgage would benefit the family's other real estate investments, she agreed that it was a good idea.

Unfortunately, after interest rates went up, the transaction had to be put on hold until rates come down again.

Isaak

Children can become the beneficiaries of their parents' accumulated equity while their parents are still around. Like it was in the case of Isaak. He got himself into financial trouble and asked his ninety-two-year-old mom for help. Instead of giving him money, she offered him the equity in her home. Since mom had limited income, the solution was a reverse mortgage L/C. I ran the scenario, which you can see in the addendum. However, Isaak's brother objected to the whole idea, and Isaak was forced to look for another solution.

CHAPTER 11

How Much it Costs

One of the concerns potential borrowers express is the cost associated with getting a reverse mortgage. The major component of the cost is the upfront mortgage insurance premium (MIP) charged on the FHA HECM loans (jumbo loans do not have MIP). Mortgage insurance is a necessary part of risky lending for either conventional or reverse mortgage loans. MIP protects the lender in the event that the Reverse Mortgage balance exceeds the property value when the loan is repaid. It has two parts: upfront and monthly charges. The upfront fee, which is 2% of the highest available amount, is usually added to the loan amount. It can be paid by the borrowers, but usually it is not. You can see the breakdown in the Addendum. After the principal limit (based on the various programs) is calculated by the computer, the cost is subtracted. It consists of three components, (two in Jumbo loans) the Initial Mortgage Insurance Premium, the Origination Fee, and other costs (which are basically title, escrow, recording, and other fees). The balance amount is the Available Principal Limit. Since these costs are financed, they will increase the balance of the loan (ie there will be no out-of-pocket expense to the borrower). This amount plus accrued interest will come due at the time of sale or refinance of the property. Regardless of the reason, the value of the property is going to be higher or lower depending on outside factors, like appreciation.

Besides the costs I've mentioned, which are financed, there are other associated costs to be paid from the borrowers' own pockets. Except for the cost of counselling services for reverse mortgages, which are about $150, the other costs are similar to conventional mortgages. The credit report and appraisal fees, which can amount to $1,000, are also charged to the borrower's credit card prior to closing. There can also be costs that relate to the safety of the residence. When the appraiser does his or her inspection, they must verify that the appliances are working and that there are no health and safety concerns that need repairs to make the residence safe.

California, and perhaps other states, require the installation of smoke detectors on each floor outside each bedroom area. It also requires one Carbon Monoxide Alarm per floor. In our home, we had smoke detectors installed long ago. Therefore, before the appraiser came to our house, I bought a few Carbon Monoxide detectors at Costco for about $25. These did not require installation. You can buy a unit that will have both alarms and can be affixed to the ceiling. The water heater tank must be double strapped to the wall. All construction, painting, and repair work has to be completed, and debris has to be removed. As I shared with you before, some of my clients had to hire contractors, which definitely added to their costs.

CHAPTER 12
Last Stories

As I neared the end of the writing of this book, I thought that I had covered enough ground and described a sufficient number of cases to show you how some of my clients found ways to enjoy their retirement, and then my associate Gerry began helping a client who had an unfortunate set of circumstances; and I came across more stories to share.

Sam

Sam was in his early eighties and had a successful career as an attorney. He owned his home, had a second home, and was enjoying his retirement. Together with his partner, he took a cruise, during which both of them contracted COVID-19. Unfortunately, the partner died. Sam had difficulty recovering and required in-home support. Concerned that he would not be able to handle his monthly financial obligations, he decided to take out a reverse mortgage. As a result, his conventional mortgage and line of credit were paid off. Now he has no monthly mortgage payments and an extra $50,000 in a line of credit that will continue to increase if he does not use it.

This story serves to show that many retirees need unexpected help that could be obtained from a reverse mortgage. It is my job to assist these people, and it's the reason I wrote this book.

While working on the editing of this book, I came across four new clients, whose circumstances might add to other stories showing how a reverse mortgage can help you or someone you know enjoy retirement.

The first call came from a woman whose husband had recently become permanently disabled. Though she was working part-time, his social security of $1,700 a month was not enough to handle their mortgage payments. There were other legal issues related to the fact that she was not the co-owner of the house, which I had to deal with as part of the process of securing a new reverse mortgage.

The next situation was indirect. I was in the process of securing a construction loan for a client. During our conversation, reverse mortgages were mentioned. "Can you get one in New York?" the client asked. It turns out that his sister was selling her home in the suburbs of New York. There were no buyers, and with a limited income, she could barely make the monthly payments. Additionally, selling the home would trigger at least a 30 percent capital gains tax. After checking the numbers, the answer was that a reverse mortgage would not only refinance her current mortgage, but it would also give her a substantial line of credit. As a result, she did not have to sell her home.

The next inquiry about reverse mortgages came up during our recent visit to North Carolina, where we stayed with friends, Carla and Richard. When I mentioned reverse mortgages to Richard, he told me that a reverse mortgage is a bad program, and he repeated all of the negative misinformation one typically hears about it. Nevertheless, when I explained to him how it really works, he asked how he could get one. Richard is seventy-six; however, his wife, Carla, is only sixty. The reason for his change of heart was that he did not want to deplete his retirement 401K account.

On our recent vacation, I received a phone call from a woman. She had been referred to me by her uncle, a client I had helped secure a reverse mortgage for many years earlier. This call was about her mother, my client's sister, who was going to be ninety-four. Her mom, who was getting in-home-support services that cost $19,000 every month, was running out of money. After checking her options, I found that I would be able to help her get about a $750,000 reverse mortgage line of credit.

These developments prompted me to think about all people; not just in California, who need my assistance. As a result, I decided to get licensed in other states as well. So far, I am in the process of getting licensed in Arizona, Colorado, Nevada, New York, North Carolina, and Oregon. And I plan to continue to get licenses from other states. When I studied for the Arizona license exam, I found out that 21 percent of FHA loans taken by borrowers are reverse mortgages. It seems that more people are moving from expensive states like California to other states where they can afford to retire. Reverse mortgages can be part of this strategy.

AFTERWORD

When I began writing this book, my intent was to share with you how a reverse mortgage can help some people retire and enjoy their lives. To educate myself and find out what was written on the subject, I checked with the public library and found many books that had the term "reverse mortgage" in their titles. I was not surprised that all of them covered what reverse mortgages are, the different types of reverse mortgages, and how they work. Certainly, this is important information when one is trying to understand the topic. One of the books, specifically written for financial advisors, asked the question, "Why are a growing number of advisors embracing and endorsing the reverse mortgage?" In the References section, I list all the books I consulted, just in case you decide to educate yourself further on this topic.

Though you might find a lot of fine details, regardless of whether you're talking about a reverse mortgage, a line of credit, or a home equity investment (HEI), I suggest finding a mortgage professional you trust. She or he will help find the solution that will help you enjoy your retirement.

The mission of my life is to help other people better theirs. I have many gifts that I enjoy sharing with others. One of them is finding mortgage solutions, but I am also a photo artist and I write and publish photo books. My latest projects are the "42 Encounters" series photobooks. This is why I decided to include photos of nature and people enjoying it in this book as well. After all, regardless of if you are retired or not, you might be reminded to enjoy the beauty of the world around us.

In addition to the books I've published, I recently designed a website focused on people who need some healing: thehealingimages.com. I believe that people who buy my images of beautiful flowers and then meditate on them will feel a sense of relaxation that may contribute to faster healing. On this site, you will also be able to buy my books.

At the end of this book, in the Addendum, you will find an example of the information that clients receive at the beginning of the reverse mortgage application that would come along with many pages describing what to know and what to expect from the reverse mortgage process that the Loan Originator would deliver to the borrower. The information can be overwhelming. Therefore, plan on finding a good guide to help you navigate through the process.

Please enjoy your retirement and share love!

ADDENDUM

There are various costs associated with getting any mortgage, and as with conventional loans, the cost varies depending on the type of loan. This is why I am including the disclosure that borrowers receive at the start of the reverse mortgage application process. You can see that there are four different options, and each of them has a lot of confusing numbers. All four came from the same lender. Since there are many lenders who offer reverse mortgages, each might have slightly different options. The highest dollar amount is the initial mortgage insurance premium (IMIP) of $21,786 (shown in the first two columns). There is also the monthly insurance premium (MIP), 0.50 percent of which is added to the interest rate to calculate monthly payments, which borrowers can choose to pay or not. Then there is the origination fee, which is paid to a mortgage loan originator (MLO, such as me). The other costs are closing costs. In the Estimate of Closing Cost worksheet, you can see that all of these costs are subtracted from the loan amount, which is calculated by the program's software and will depend on the appraised value of the property. Borrowers are expected to review the proposal, read all the pages describing a reverse mortgage, and then get reverse mortgage counseling. In California, seven days later, loan originators can order an appraisal report and a credit report. Both are paid for with the borrower's credit card. This is the only upfront charge. The cost of the appraisal report may vary depending on the value and type of property, since reverse mortgages can also be done for one- to four-unit buildings, as well as condominiums.

The presentation package also includes an amortization schedule, which will vary depending on the chosen program. It assumes that the value of the property will continue to increase by 4 percent per year. The schedule extends to a proposed client's age of ninety-nine, and as you can see in the given example where the borrower was ninety-two, after eight years, it is still expected that there will be equity for the heirs to inherit.

Learn More...

Add Product

	CMT Mo 5 B Finance of America Revers	HECM Fixed B Finance of America Revers	HS Select 4.0 Finance of America Revers	HomeSafe Finance of America Revers
Index	1YrTBill	N/A	1YrTBill	N/A
Margin	2.375	N/A	6.875	N/A
Initial Rate	7.175%	6.560	11.675%	9.740
Expected Rate	5.955%	6.560%	11.675%	9.740%
MIP	0.50%	0.50%	N/A	N/A
Cap on Interest Rate	12.175%	6.560%	16.675%	9.740%
Monthly Servicing Fee	$0.00	$0.00	$20.00	$0.00
Initial LOC Growth	7.675%	N/A	1.500%	N/A
Home Value	$1,300,000.00	$1,300,000.00	$1,300,000.00	$1,300,000.00
Lending Limit	$1,089,300.00	$1,089,300.00	N/A	N/A
Max. Claim Amount	$1,089,300.00	$1,089,300.00	$1,300,000.00	$1,300,000.00
Principal Limit	$708,045.00	$691,705.50	$668,200.00	$668,200.00
- Servicing Fee Set Aside	$0.00	$0.00	N/A	N/A
Adjusted Principal Limit	$708,045.00	$691,705.50	$668,200.00	$668,200.00
- IMIP	$21,786.00	$21,786.00	N/A	N/A
- Origination Fee	$6,000.00	$6,000.00	$19,500.00	$6,682.00
- Other Costs	$3,803.14	$3,803.14	$4,544.14	$4,544.14
+ Credits	$0.00	$0.00	$0.00	$0.00
Remaining Principal Limit	$676,455.86	$660,116.36	$644,155.86	$656,973.86
- Liens and Mortgages	$0.00	$0.00	$0.00	$0.00
- Repair Set Aside	$0.00	$0.00	$0.00	$0.00
Property Charge Set Aside Type	Not Required	Not Required	Not Required	Not Required
1st Year Property Charge Set Aside Total	$0.00	$0.00	$0.00	$0.00
Additional Property Charge Set Aside	$0.00	$0.00	$0.00	$0.00
- Total Property Charge Set Aside	$0.00	$0.00	$0.00	$0.00
Available Principal Limit	$676,455.86	$660,116.36	$644,155.86	$656,973.86
Funds Available at Closing	$393,237.86	$383,434.16	$577,335.86	$656,973.86
Monthly Tenure During 1st Year	$8,991.85	N/A	N/A	N/A
Monthly Tenure Available	$8,991.85	N/A	N/A	N/A
Cash Request	$393,237.86	$383,434.16	$577,335.86	$656,973.86
Monthly Payment During 1st Year	$0.00	N/A	N/A	N/A
Monthly Payment Request	$0.00	N/A	N/A	N/A
Line Of Credit Available 1st Year	$0.00	N/A	$66,820.00	N/A
Additional Line Of Credit Available After 1st Year	$283,218.00	N/A	$0.00	N/A
Total Line Of Credit Available	$283,218.00	N/A	$66,820.00	N/A
Cap Initial Disbursement Limit at Low IMIP	☐	☐	☐	☐
Total Mandatory Obligations	$31,589.14	$31,589.14	N/A	N/A
% of Principal Limit	4.47%	4.57%	N/A	N/A
Initial Disbursement Limit	$424,827.00	$415,023.30	N/A	N/A
% of Principal Limit	60.00%	60.00%	N/A	N/A
Initial Loan Balance (UPB)	$424,827.00	$415,023.30	$601,380.00	$668,200.00
% of Principal Limit	60.00%	60.00%	90.00%	100.00%
Single Disbursement Lump Sum Option	☐	☑	☐	
Unavailable Principal Limit	$0.00	$276,682.20	$0.00	$0.00

Estimate of Closing Costs Worksheet

Date: **April 25, 2023** Estimated Home Value: **$1,300,000.00**
Prepared For:

Property Address:

This is not a Good Faith Estimate or a Truth-in-Lending Disclosure Statement required by federal law. If you make an application with us, your Good Faith Estimate and Truth-in-Lending Disclosure Statement will be provided to you in the opening package. This is not a commitment to lend, nor is it a rate lock, pre-qualification or pre-approval. This worksheet is intended to assist you in evaluating a loan or home purchase using estimated closing and property costs. Closing and settlement costs, reserve deposits, interest rate and Annual Percentage Rate (APR) are subject to change and the estimates shown below may be more or less depending on factors such as down payment, property type, and occupancy. Housing costs will vary depending on location, homeowner's association dues, local and state fees, taxes, and hazard and mortgage insurance. Charges from third parties, which may include Lender's affiliates, will be passed through at the actual cost charged by the third party. You should review these estimated charges when considering the total cost of your loan.

Estimated Closing Costs

Finance Charges	**POC Amount**	**Estimated Amount**
Counseling fee	$125.00	
MERS registration		$24.95
Mortgage Insurance Premium		$21,786.00
Origination Fee		$2,250.00
Settlement or closing fee		$550.00
Tax Cert Fee		$50.00
Other Charges		
Notary/Signing Fee		$400.00
Appraisal fee		$550.00
Broker Compensation (paid by lender to broker: $10,738.32)		
Credit report		$45.19
Document preparation		$140.00
Flood certification		$20.00
Lender's title insurance		$2,148.00
Recording charges mortgage		$425.00
	$125.00	$28,389.14
Total Estimated Settlement Costs		$28,514.14

Loan Officer Company NMLS #: 196454
2006-2023 ReverseVision, Inc. 4611,644 Page 1 of 1 Printed: 4/25/2023 EstimateOfClosingCosts / 0677

Amortization Schedule - Annual Projections

Borrower Name/Case Number:		Refinance:	No
Age of Youngest Borrower:	92	Beg. Mortgage Balance:	$405,219.60
Interest Rate (Expected / Initial):	6.990% / 6.990%	Expected Appreciation:	4.000%
Maximum Claim Amount:	$1,089,300.00	Initial Line Of Credit:	$0.00
Initial Principal Limit:	$675,366.00	Monthly Payment:	$0.00
Initial Advance:	$376,830.46	Monthly Servicing Fee:	$0.00
Lien Payoffs with Reverse Mortgage:	$0.00	Mortgage Insurance (MIP)	0.50%
Financed Closing Costs:	$28,389.14	Life Expectancy Set-Aside:	$0.00
Initial Property Value:	$1,300,000.00	LESA Semi-annual Disbursement:	$0.00

NOTE: Actual interest charges and property value projections may vary from amounts shown. Available credit will be less than projected if funds are withdrawn from a line of credit (LOC). Additionally, the Cash Payment column below reflects annual disbursements from both a LOC and a LESA, if applicable.

		Annual Totals					End of Year Projections			
Yr	Age	SVC Fee	Cash Payment	MIP	Rate	Interest	Loan Balance	Line Of Credit	Property Value	Equity
1	92	$0	$0	$2,097	6.990%	$29,318	$436,634	$0	$1,352,000	$915,241
2	93	$0	$0	$2,260	6.990%	$31,591	$470,485	$0	$1,406,080	$935,470
3	94	$0	$0	$2,435	6.990%	$34,040	$506,959	$0	$1,462,323	$955,239
4	95	$0	$0	$2,624	6.990%	$36,679	$546,262	$0	$1,520,816	$974,430
5	96	$0	$0	$2,827	6.990%	$39,522	$588,611	$0	$1,581,649	$992,913
6	97	$0	$0	$3,046	6.990%	$42,586	$634,243	$0	$1,644,915	$1,010,547
7	98	$0	$0	$3,282	6.990%	$45,888	$683,413	$0	$1,710,711	$1,027,173
8	99	$0	$0	$3,537	6.990%	$49,445	$736,395	$0	$1,779,140	$1,042,620

Date

Loan Officer Company NMLS #: 196454

 4611,644

Page 1 of 1

Printed: 4/25/2023
AMORT/ 0285

EXPRESSIONS OF GRATITUDE

This book was possible because so many of my clients gave me the opportunity to assist them at the start of a new chapter in their lives—retirement. All of the stories are real. Initially, I had planned to use fictitious names for the clients whose stories I present, but when I shared this project with my clients, surprisingly some wanted me to use their real names to make them "famous." I am going to list those whom I was able to assist, in the order that they appear in the book, to show how diverse the circumstances can be and how these retirees were helped.

Igor and Margarita: Were able to buy a home in Pittsburg, California, with a reverse mortgage, and to refinance it three years later to lower their mortgage insurance premium.

Paul: After retirement, his home needed improvement. We tried a reverse mortgage and ended up with conventional refinancing.

Bob and Angela: Had high medical expenses, got a reverse mortgage with cash-out. Two years later, they refinanced the reverse mortgage for an additional amount of cash-out.

John and Tom: Three partners inherited one property; two partners bought out the third partner with a reverse mortgage.

Roger: Could not get a reverse mortgage because of the property condition, was declined by the HEI program, but was able to get a private money loan.

Fred: After retirement, paid off his existing mortgage through a reverse mortgage.

Mike: Was disabled in retirement and inherited a property. A reverse mortgage paid off the existing mortgage with additional cash-out.

Dave and Hanna: Inherited a house with an existing reverse mortgage. Refinanced the property with a new reverse mortgage.

Clara: After retirement, received a reverse mortgage with cash-out. Two years later, refinanced into a new reverse mortgage with cash-out.

John and Greta: Retired and got a reverse mortgage. After selling their office building, they later refinanced using a reverse mortgage with an additional cash-out to pay off capital gains.

Beatrice: Originally received a mortgage after a condo conversion. After the condo was sold, she purchased a new home for cash, after which, she took a Reverse mortgage line of credit.

Natalie and George: After her husband's death, Natalie received a reverse mortgage line of credit.

Nancy: After semi-retirement, she could not get a reverse mortgage because of her condo's limitations, however she qualified for a HEI.

Andrey and Olga: Used an HEI as a bridge loan to buy a property in Sacramento, California, with an unconventional purchase loan. They later refinanced into a reverse mortgage.

Linda: Had issues with her health. She was offered an HEI and reverse mortgage and has chose a HEI.

Greg and Jenny: Attempted to refinance an apartment building but then switched to a reverse mortgage. Eventually they put everything on hold.

Sam: Suffered health complications from COVID-19; after the death of his partner, he got a reverse mortgage with a line of credit.

...

Of course, I want to thank those wonderful people who helped me put this book together:

Vladimir Rodstein who, through many years of working together, has learned to understand my handwritten manuscripts and makes them readable for others.

Amy Bauman who reviews all my books and makes them understandable.

Jeni Shindorf who uses her artistic skills to put this book together and designs book covers, utilizing my photo-images.

Dennis Polyak who did the final editing.

Alona Kagan, my daughter, the author of the book "The Weaver", who helped me choose the correct images for each page and made the final review.

BIBLIOGRAPHY

Accola, Harlan J. (2018) 'Home Equity and Reverse Mortgages:' The Cinderella of the Baby Boomer Retirement, Better Way to Live, Inc., A Marshfield WI

Anderson, Jim (2012) 'Reverse Mortgage Dangers:' The Pros, Cons, Drawbacks, Downsides and Disadvantages, Lions Pride Publishing, LLC, Green Valley, AZ

Barlow, John (2015) 'Understanding Reverse Mortgages:' Increase Your Cash Flow and Minimize Your Stress!, Merrell Publishing Company, LLC, Seattle, WA

Bhuyan, Vishaal B. (2011) 'AARP Reverse Mortgages and Linked Securities:' The Complete Guide to Risk, Pricing and Regulation, John Wiley and Sons

Boroson, Warren (2006) 'The Reverse Mortgage Advantage: ' The Tax-Free, House-Rich Way to Retire Wealthy, McGraw Hill LLC

Foxx, Rick (2020) 'Reverse Mortgages Made Simple!', Foxx Media, USA

Galloway, Meghan and Kantor, Richard, Editors (2013) 'Reverse Mortgages:' Elements, Considerations and Marketing Developments, Nova Science Pub Inc; UK

Giordano, Shelly (2015) 'What's the Deal with Reverse Mortgages?', People Tested Media, Pennington, NJ

Graves, Don (2018) 'Housing Wealth:' 3 Ways the New Reverse Mortgage Is Changing Retirement Income Conversations (An Advisor's Guide), Housing Wealth Institute

Graves, Don (2019) 'The Retiree Guide to Housing Wealth:' 5 Ways the New Reverse Mortgage Is Changing Retirement, Housing Wealth Institute

Holcomb, Cindy (2008) 'The Reverse Mortgage Book' Everything You Need to Know Explained Simply, Atlantic Publishing Group Inc., Ocala, FL

Hostler, Jim (2018) 'Reverse Mortgage 360:' A New Perspective, CreateSpace Independent Publishing Platform

Hultquist, Dan (2015) 'Understanding Reverse:' Answers to 30 Common Questions—Simplifying the New Reverse Mortgage, CreateSpace, An Amazon.com Company

Kelly, Tom (2005) 'The New Reverse Mortgage Formula:' How to Convert Home Equity into Tax-Free Income, Wiley

Kraemer, Tammy and Kraemer, Tyler (2007) 'The Complete Guide to Reverse Mortgages:' Turn Your Home Equity into Instant Income!, Adams Media, Vero Beach, FL

Lucas, John E and Lyons, Sarah Glendon (2008) 'Reverse Mortgages for Dummies, Thorndike Press, Waterville ME

Patti, Greg (2006) 'Reverse Mortgages:' Cash for the Rest of Your Life!, BookSurge Publishing, USA

Pfau, Wade D. (2018) 'Reverse Mortgages:' How to Use Reverse Mortgages to Secure Your Retirement, McLean Asset Management Corporation, Tysons, VA

Ranson, Steven and Ziomecki, Yvonne (2021) 'Home Run: ' The Reverse Mortgage Advantage, FriesenPress, Pemnina, ND

Roberts, Mike (2020) 'The Reverse Mortgage Revealed:' An Industry Insider's Guide to the Reverse Mortgage, MyHECM.com

Talmadge, Jarred J. (2020) 'Too Good to Be Free:' How a Reverse Mortgage Can Improve Your Life, Your Cash Flow, and Pay You Too, Three Feet Publishing, Centennial, CO

BOOKS BY THIS AUTHOR

The Mortgage Game

From his childhood of factory work in communist Latvia to his current life as one of the Bay Area's most respected and successful mortgage industry professionals, Manny Kagan has enjoyed a colorful journey to the top. In this fascinating book, The Mortgage Game, Manny shares not only his amazing life story but also his secrets to finding the best mortgages possible. It all boils down to his trademark "Five Cs"—Collateral, Capacity, Credit, Capital and Character. Using real-life examples, Manny shows how he was able to overcome the "minuses" of some of his mortgage- or refinance-seeking clients (and most clients have some minuses) and turn them into "pluses." Just about every mortgage lender working today talks about the Four Cs, but Kagan takes it a step further and includes his own signature fifth C—character. This is the one that often makes the difference – and it's the one that helped him become a leader in the industry. In this book Kagan pulls back the curtain and shares details of his own real estate transactions—from the very first house he and his wife bought for their family, to subsequent refinance deals he was able to close on a basket of rental properties. The Mortgage Game is a valuable tool for anyone who's thinking of investing in real estate or refinancing an existing loan. The Mortgage Game offers up-to-date information on the current marketplace, along with clear explanations of how the market got itself into so much trouble. But this valuable book also offers more – it's the one reference guide every home-buyer needs.

Mortgage Solutions for Smart People™

The Mortgage Industry is an industry where the more experienced pros have a higher success rate. It is the years of connections and the experience of having been through so many loan scenarios that separate the average Mortgage Broker from the consummate professional like Manny Kagan. This is a book that is not solely technical, but also has a touch of personality. Manny discusses his roots and how he didn't start on top. He lays it all out in "Mortgage Solutions For Smart People" so that it is a science, with a methodology targeted at loan approval.

There is a difference between knowing about mortgages and writing books about the subject. Manny Kagan's published works can be found on the desks of many of the top mortgage professionals in the country. He brings this knowledge to the masses with this latest book release.

Here readers will learn about specific tools that borrowers can use to improve their chance of getting a better mortgage, or to get approved for a mortgage when they go after the American Dream.

"Mortgage Solutions for Smart People" is a book written from the heart. Manny has a writing style that makes the reader feel like they are sitting with Manny listening to his every word. No doubt that

Manny sleeps well at night, after all, he enjoys helping people, and has in fact helped some folks on repeated occasions. People come back to Manny because they know he is the real thing, a Mortgage Professional that knows how to get the job done, which in this case is having a Mortgage Loan Approved.

42 Encounters in San Francisco

In early 2015, when I decided to put together some of my images from my walks and encounters in San Francisco into a photography book, I had no idea that it would evolve into what is now my "42 Encounters" project. My plan is to create 42 books over the next 42 years; one image, one story, one book at a time. All the profits from the sales of the books will be invested in the creation of a forum to teach the young and young at heart how to see the beauty of the world through the lens of the camera or cell phone. I have great hope that you will become part of this vision as well. Buy the books, create your own collection and share this idea with your loved ones.

42 Encounters with Dog Lovers

Our labradoodle puppy Max was my present to my wife Elfa for our fiftieth wedding anniversary. After he became a member of our family, I started to record our experiences with him, as well as the behavior solutions that I learned from various books. These experiences, plus images of various dog lovers that I have photographed in the past have become the basis of this book, the second one in the series of "42 Encounters".

42 Encounters with Laughter

When I grew up in Riga, Latvia telling jokes was a way of being. Usually conversations started with the question, "Have you heard that...?" to be followed by the old or new joke. When COVID-19 started, I felt that people needed some laughter. Combining jokes with images of laughing people was the trick. Now it's your turn to laugh.

42 Encounters with Love

What is love? Does it have to be mutual? How do you express it? What is the difference between loving people and loving nature or animals? Then the question, how to make a photo book about love? My solution was to write love poems and put them together with my photography and my love for you.

WHAT SHALL I DO NEXT?

To see if you would qualify for a reverse mortgage, all you need to do is go to this website (or use the QR code below) and fill in these six bits of information with no obligation and we will get back to you with an answer for your specific scenario.

Website: "RetirementSolutions4u.com"

1. Homeowner's First and Last Names
2. Email address
3. Phone number
4. Birth date of the youngest homeowner
5. Indicate the value of your home (check Zillow)
6. Balance remaining on the mortgage

QR Code:

"Max, Elfa and Manny Kagan"

Have a happy and worry-free retirement.

Thank you for reading. You can always reach me by email.

With best wishes,

Manny Kagan

MannyKagan@comcast.net